Francine Sterle | *What Thread?*

2014 DAVID MARTINSON — MEADOWHAWK PRIZE

Francine Sterle

What Thread?

Red Dragonfly Press

ISBN 978-1-937693-79-4 paper

Library of Congress Control Number: 2015936212

Full acknowledgments printed at the back of the book

Cover photograph: 'Prayer Flags' by Francine Sterle

Designed and typeset at Red Dragonfly Press
using Athelas by José Scaglione & Veronika Burian

Printed in the United States of America
on 30% recycled stock
by BookMobile, a 100% wind-powered company

Published by Red Dragonfly Press
Press-in-Residence at the Anderson Center
P. O. Box 406
Red Wing, MN 55066

For more information and additional titles visit our website
www.reddragonflypress.org

Contents

Notes
Acknowledgments
About the Author
David Martinson–Meadowhawk Prize

To my daughter Ellie Speare

The love I have for you was with me at each turn of this journey.

I

Afterlife

"Solvitur ambulando . . . It is solved by walking."
– St. Augustine

I

Behind the silent bars
an iron thought remains

round and hard
as the ball of pitch

Theseus threw headlong
into the monster's gaping mouth,

but I cannot let it go, trapped
as it is inside

the chambered maze
I've made of my heart.

2

This is what I recall:
marsh marigold, water willow, meadow rue—

not the puddle of blood
you left on the bed

nor the white-boned buttons
torn from your chest

nor even that box of wasps
buzzing madly

deep in the barn
nesting in the damp rot

where I first walked
bare-armed without you.

3

It begins with a finger of water
then a brook, a stream, a pond—

filling—till you were covered over
like weeds in lake water.

You simply disappeared:
the current pulling you

as your mind swayed this way
and that, this way

and that.

4

A low, polar sun sets
over a honeycomb of tunnels
dissolved out of limestone layers

while I speak to you in shouts
against an otherworldly wind
racing through the pass.

Across this momentous divide,
it is a long vigil I keep
against the ebbing light of winter.

5

The way the scar slept on your body.

The way I followed its visible ridge
as if it were a promontory.

The way I stood looking out
high above coastal waters.

How far it would be when I fell.

6

Seasons change;
      landscapes change;
            language falters—

but I'll never escape
      the starched bed,
            your barely breathing frame,

the night nurse's
      morphine
            drip.

7

Enlaced in the ruins,
I ask a question.

Perception answers,
an artifact at a time.

Digging deeper:
debris and decay.

There were so many signs of unknowing.
I spent years on my knees in that dirt.

8

While it was happening—
rain taking the shape of a wave
waves slapping the shoreline of sleep—

salvation's boat
appeared and disappeared, appeared
then disappeared.

Blowing in from the sea,
a steady headwind surged
over the rolling tidewater
as it bounced beneath me.

Shreds of dead seaweed
wrapped around my legs.

Abyss of the examined life.

The storm gathered and expanded
as the shipwrecked world tossed me to and fro,
the end already set in motion.

9

That final night
your empty shoes
stood watch beside the bed.

What turn will it add to the labyrinth?
What thread?

10

And then absence arrived:
a rivulet disappearing into rock,

a living space but empty
geometry to the eye.

House that fear makes.

Who tiptoes in the next room?

Air without your face, your name?
Shadow that will never let me go?

I contended for you.
I did not waver.

The cry you hear is mine, and numb.

II

Because the body persists,
you walk into the house

wings so wide
down goes the glass

vase of cushion mums
drained of color

while a kitchen knife
slides from my lap like a sleigh.

12

An angel made new
collapses,

the astral world folding in

like nastic petals
closing at nightfall.

Seraphim, cherubim and thrones
tumble from the sky.

And then you,
ghostly herald at the bidding of—
give way.

13

Why stand out in the uncreated?

This is no blind act
but a desperate step
out of a benighted world

where a ragged orchid
begins to unfold
its deeply lacerated lip.

14

What the wall says.

What the wall says
at 3 a.m.
when mourning is disordered.

Defaced, it's a weapon.

Washed white,
a visage comes to itself.

It seeks meaning elsewhere
or nowhere.

Sharp gulps of mercurial air.

15

Sound keeps coming up through the stones.
You, who are no longer flesh,
who cannot find your way.

As if on horseback,
spirited reins flying,
hoof-beats thundering in my ear.

And the uncertain dust.
Clouds of it
kicking up.

The road is a spine broken where it curves.

After years of it,
a flattened path.
Ridden forth
with nothing left untouched.

16

Brought to the brooding yews
    above which flies
        a satin-black bird
            in circles:

a mandala, a dervish,
    calligraphy in air
        loosening
            as little by little

a sudden pitch of vertigo
    plunges me into adjacent space
        where every missed exit,
            every degree of beatitude

reels past; thus, the world
    and the impalpable blank
        every grieving person
            fears it will become.

17

I have a life to go home to...

Forse che sì, forse che no...

18

Count the days.
All the same and all different.

Hours made of air
leave fistfuls of ash at my feet.

With every breath of air,
a shiver in what I see,

what I think I see:
phantom who will never let me go,

who possesses the trembling trees,
the darkened house,

who hovers at my door,
making sound out of silence.

19

Because whatever I expected
wasn't there, I draw back

and catch the wind's
razor cut on my cheek:

the same wind that plays with mirrors
turns the pages on the street.

20

As if from darkness—
cold-blooded and secluded—

as if from the heart's tomb
or a cave formed below
a sharp ridge of rocks,

its entrance
narrowing behind me.

As if from the pillared cloister.

As if emergence were everything.

21

Over and over
a muffled cadence
each time my foot—
its operatic journey—
picks itself up.

One step might be a cliché,
but my feet won't stop

repeating the sound
Mnemosyne makes as she

retells her story
again and again and again.

22

From a stand of maples
fired with autumn,

the urgent, twirling leaves
fly off into a spiral of wind.

If you have not entered the dance,
you mistake the event...

but, the mess of death
refuses to let go.

This is madness—
        ask Ariadne.

How many crane dances must I do?

23

Your body once again:
two black crescent moons
under your eyes.

Between embraces,
the shadows clear.

Ribbons fall down my back
like strings of rain.

24

From well-fed flowers
to the wrecked bouquet.

The beatitudes of form
impose their tide.

Pausing between two worlds,
I give myself over,

the floating moon
variable but bright.

25

Bend after bend
but leading to what?

Axis mundi?
As above, so below?

When two poles intersect,
the soul glides.

A voice is optional.

There's nothing esoteric about that.

26

All these days
I am blind and travel alone.

What lives on in me.
What I have made of it.

The gravel road,
narrow as a monkey's tail,
comes alive beneath my feet.

Near the ghat where they burn the dead,
I falter when I see
the first body set aflame.

27

Like a snowflake
stitched on a bed quilt
or a hopscotch pitch
chalked upon the pavement,

there are hard angles,
arrays of halls,
crypts, corridors,
blind walls,
circuits reinventing themselves.

It's a frightening game
without any words:

the experience within,
the view from without.

28

If I fail it is enough
to have come to the water:

gray sea-sway,
a far-off island
blotted by driving rain.

The foreground is fog and confusion.
Spume and seawater.
Seaweed and shifting sand.

How long before the sinking?
How far to the broken cliffs?

29

Of love, no less.
Seven days of rain.
My thoughts flood the field,
wash away the boat on the water.

Waves of intent.

As I plunge into the swell,
a high-pitched mewing
arrives from the other shore.

A gray-mantled gull dips
to a pencil-line of water.
Is there any distance
it cannot cross?

30

Beyond vine-strung boulders,
a path at long last

through choked undergrowth,
over deceptive layers of moss,

across a rocky outcrop,
where knots of creeping tree roots
lead me on my uneven way.

Without warning, the sad
lunar voice of evening
breaks free from the nightbird's song.

It can't be taken back.

31

Where the road swings west,
a rare halo of light.

Everything in circles.

The molecules of my body
vibrate like a swirling nebula:
a rhythm I cannot direct
but am directed by.

A complicated constellation.

A direction
I finally choose to follow.

32

Where do I reside but here?
Geography without consequence.

A patch of black grass
dwindles beneath me.

Do not call it fixity.

If I look long enough
the scene landscapes me.

The small vault of my ribs.
The canopy of heaven.

33

Over time
the meridians rearrange themselves,

pass through
the body's celestial sphere,

bend the pathways
along which I've stumbled

over each human hurdle.

34

Among flower pools, clouds of water,
the pink-finned fish.

Alone with my slippery thoughts
which go everywhere

and nowhere, which waver
between silence and meaning.

I cannot catch them.

Little ruffles in the water.
The body both real and unreal.

The holiness of the body
both entering and leaving.

Long hours of attention.
Attention until there is absence,

and the veil parts.

II

[now begins]

now begins an impossible journey
        now a meandering line appears
            now disappears

something unravels
        something inside
            something missing

this morning
        watching a streak-backed bird
            land in brackish water

for the first time
        I saw before me
            what cannot be measured in miles

again the absence
        [again] the round wind
            again the circling

across a gray plane of sky
        from restless clouds
            a long-awaited rain

the world is full of signs
        the day's disorder
            a thousand times repeated

a thread on the ground
        a vine-choked garden
            a garland of games

but there's a barrier—
    and a little bruise to the land
        where I have thrown myself down

[journey on foot from any direction]

journey on foot from any direction
    you might be years on the same path
        before seeking

the opposite direction—
    caves and quarries
        arches of thorn

sinuosities   nobody knew   existed

here   every terrible thing is possible

    they've made a curse of this maze
        no words for what you might find

forget the romantic hedge puzzle
    where red-cheeked children   or trysting lovers
        weave along well-groomed alleys of yew—

    it's death practicing her steps
and fortified walls   massive   as Troy's   topless towers
    where   doubtful turns   unravel
like the shifting stories   History offers

    the tangled landscape   overlaps   then traps

    this prison is yours if you dare

[darest thou now?]

    courage is careless

    the same hell wherever you start from...

[how much of the map]

how much of the map
        could be labeled
                terra incognita

how much   unknown   invisible to others
      how much of myself   could I shake off
abandon   those undiscovered places
        [I barely know]   exist

    though the map is not the territory
how I am drawn   to leave behind the pattern
         for the path   for a minute
             an hour   for one whole day
I'd be like a Wintu   describing the body
       using cardinal directions

he touches me on the west arm
                the river is to the east
       when we return   *his east arm*
circles around me   *and the river*
         stays to the west

      without that landscape   to connect to
   who am I   apart from what surrounds me

at the edge of the unknown   dirt
      unceasingly does my thinking
         in bonam/malem partem
until it is a smooth stone in my mouth

venturing forward   doubling back
        what I see   depends on where I am

if there be death
    if the dark night of the soul
        O, I know what is waiting

every threshold is sacred
    the eternal allure
        of what comes next

[what about the corridors]

what about the corridors
        of our own construction
                [the ones labeled

lust, treachery, deceit]
        inside which
                the Minotaur fattens?

error and entrapment
        choices
                that become a way of life

the packed earth
        collapses without warning
                a railless abyss

and on the horizon
        more abyss   give me
                a clew of thread and a sword

till the stink of the monster
        is upon me
                and the beating heart

quickens to hear
        the horned animal's
                hoof-footed cries

[another kind of awake]

another kind of awake
        dirty tail of a cloud
                rising from dusty feet

the rat-alley stench
        discarded needles
                bits of blown debris

[pick your way through if you can]
        no way out of the filthy darkness
                the world around me wears

no matter which way I turn
        razor wire
                a nightly excursion in Hell

cockroaches dart past me
        a jangled chord
                high-pitched from my mouth

if I were a girl again
        there'd be a liturgical medal
                pinned to my shirt

Dear God, what is there to do
        at a time like this, on an avenue
                this dreary, in a city this lost—

wind sharpens its teeth
        but I declare my sentence
                and move forward

certain things have to be 'undergone'
    and, yes, those
            who go unguided wander

[whoever dropped the grain on my path]

whoever dropped
        the grain on my path

whoever   came before

        whoever insisted
    courage wasn't enough

            forgive me

how could I escape
    fortune's uncertainties   without you

            our lot
    falls to us   without explanation

faith loses its way
        as the double-headed axe
                drops one way or another

fear loses its way   as I play
        hide and seek
                [life's fragile game]
inside this murderous maze

[straight ahead]

versantem turbine leti

straight ahead   a thousand yards
  through the sand's   timeless grip on this desert
there's a formal court   opening   like a lotus
   revealing dozens more   enclosed by wide walls
  doors running   opposite one another   every choice
    crisscrossed with passages   disappearing
along continuously curving ramps   inclined toward heaven
toward porches   where flights of marble stairs
    plummet underground   to colossal rooms
three thousand or more   some hollow places   grim
  as a confessional   my internal compass   spinning as I race
from court to room   room to hall   down tight corridors
  from other halls   to other courts   past colonnades
  endless turnings   identical doors   set in vaulted walls
   but not showing the way   so back again
retracing my steps   always   in the dark
  the constant errors   the crypts   the subterranean tunnels
   the intricately carved temples to the gods
    twisting steps   a city of dead ends
   imposing one devious circle upon another
    the exhausted dismay of it all
  each weighty choice   inescapable
each baffling passage   trapping   the wary traveler
  and always leading   [how can it be otherwise]
    to Catullus   to his whirly whirl of death

[snaking inward]

snaking inward   concentric   semi-circles of rough cliffs
    repeating their dizzying heights   round and round
        the constant   convolutions and reversals
    disorienting   even the most cautious walker

    why have I come   who forces this entrance
      into a world reduced to spiraling rock

if the pendulous passage   leads like a dance
    stamped out on a dirt floor   to an isolating center
    to da Vinci's   octagonal room   fitted with towering mirrors
where you can see yourself   infinitely   from all sides
    where every gesture   multiplies obsessively
    in sacred   geometric space   I still might
time and again   mistake what I'm dealing with
    a place of confrontation
an undeniable underworld   mimicking bowels or brains

    beware the intricate path
    deceptively turning   back on itself
the twisting thread   with its laborious circuits   confusions   misgivings
    always ends   at the beginning

    [what is the duration of a step?
      as I move so at length I will be?]

what you depart from is not the way
    but the gods
      must I be reminded
stride forth to be followed...

[rain frog   thorn bug   tent bat]

rain frog   thorn bug   tent bat
along a broken mosaic   a spongy   ever-dwindling path
soaring trees   woody buttresses   their massive twisted fins
lofty crowns   shoulder to shoulder   climbing lime-green
vines   restless palms   one strangling plant   clinging to
choking another   a discontinuous canopy of branches and leaves
impenetrable   alive and teeming   tangled underbrush
the deeply shaded soil   lumpy roots   writhing
across the forest floor   low-growing ferns   seedlings
struggling for light   jewel-colored hummingbirds
insects sizzling and clicking and the dripping water
trickling into the tiniest of crevices   steamy
claustrophobic air   a dazzling bellbird   lost
in a shaft of sunlight   a golden eyelash viper
sinuous as a vein on a broad-leafed frond   flat worms
land leeches   walnut-sized spiders   goliath beetles
camouflaged butterflies on dead leaves   parasites   bees
leaf-cutting ants atop glorious white lilies   everywhere
gripping   climbing   twisting   floating through the trees
stilt-like aerial roots   the mouth-amazed pitcher plant
buried larvae   fruit-eating fish   the perpetual battle to adapt
the ruthless drive   to survive under a punishing sun
what grows   bursts forth at astonishing speed   then decomposes
to be reabsorbed   so much unknown   unfamiliar
unnamed   but before long   the trees seem the same
the rocks   every bird track   who would dare think of such a place
who would dare   construct one   of his own imagining
and be utterly abandoned   in the middle of it all
if to be lost is to be fully present   if confusion becomes
the only boundary   and then   the decision   [to divide space
until a direction is created]   only a madman would begin

thought is its own cage   the mind   already anticipating
the first step   deciding   every turn will be coupled
by disaster   and perhaps   some bestial creature
crouched at the center   crying   waiting
for our hero   our everyman   our Elijah wandering the earth in rags

[dust in the mouth]

dust in the mouth   dust   in every crevice
   the soldier   undone by war   the restless wanderer
the believer on his knees   crawling   in pilgrimage
  as if in a dream   as if life were a rite of passage

and along the way   serpent-footed fiends   sphinxes
   bewitching sirens   guarding   sanctuaries and cemeteries
warning or threatening   their fearsome strength   pulling me
joints   sinews   muscles   the thoughts in my head
teeming with demons   the passage getting narrower
   as I bend and stoop   my body a question mark
 into a reduced world   then   between two worlds
unable to go back   but   back to what?—

the crushing weight of the gods
      their Olympian bodies
           the sculpted rustle of drapery
the unblemished wings of their noses
      foreheads unfurrowed by age?—

back to when even the wounded
wore fixed, archaic smiles?
when appeasement was simple?—

          One jar of honey for the gods
          One jar for the keeper of the maze

if I returned   [like all who do]   I'd be more lost
    not by the act of returning   but
by becoming   someone else in the process

III

Kōan (1)

<u>Pointer:</u>

Once the arrow leaves the archer there is no return. No power to return. Trying, you will lose your balance. Step away. Give evidence to your actions.

<u>Case:</u>

Ming Chi asked Ch'ao Lin, "How far must I walk in one direction before I know where I am going?" Ch'ao Lin replied, "You have fallen into the weeds."

<u>Notes:</u>

1. Look under your feet! The path starts there.
2. A well-shot arrow does not hit anywhere.
3. The quiver is also the point.
4. He's already fallen deep in the weeds. He cannot avoid losing his bowstring.
5. The only crime is to ask the wrong question.
6. It is futile to try to take back a shot.

<u>Verse:</u>

> Geese in the sky:
>   a sudden arrow
>   of inspiration.

> Clouds
>   thick as cream
>   have not yet come together.

Kōan (2)

Pointer:

Ten thousand lightning bugs determine how you will judge
the moon. Without any further information, you cannot take
another lesson. To understand transcendence, look past the
night sky.

Case:

A monk asked Lung Shan, "When light and dark arrive, how
can we avoid them?"
Shan replied, "One must go to the place where there is no light
or dark."
The monk said, "Each day begins in light and ends in
darkness."
To which Shan said, "The ancients saw everything equally."

Notes:

1. The moon is right on your face. Where are you?
2. Don't go mistaking one moment for the next.
3. There is appearing in the world, and there is not
   appearing in the world.
4. If you reach this realm, take another lesson.

Commentary:

When it's light, the light blinds you. When it's dark, the dark
blinds you. When there is agreement, the old teacher closes
his eyes.

Verse:

As the moon takes shape
round and full,
you grasp your reflection.

See how it brightens
  the far lake,
    the leafless trees.

Kōan (3)

<u>Pointer:</u>

With every thought, a new direction. Capture the word if you want to seize the idea. That way, confusion cannot enter. When a kite makes trails in the wind, a bird's movements become manifest.

<u>Case:</u>

A monk asked Yao Yang, "How many steps before a decision is made?"
Yang said, "Look! A kite!"
The monk replied, "It's only a paper dragon."
Then Yang said, "Fire has decided to search you out."

<u>Notes:</u>

1. One thought can burn down a house. Hide your straw sandals!
2. Tell me, is this understanding or not?
3. If you cannot pass beyond it, you will be deceived by it.
4. Yao Yang changes directions with a single phrase.

<u>Commentary:</u>

Not any closer to a decision, but thinking provides a pretext. A kite takes the shape of an idea. Haven't you heard? Fire catches those who beat the bush for a bird.

<u>Verse:</u>

> Though he chased a serpent-
> tailed dragon thirty years
>
> Still it soars
> above the monk's head.
>
> In the pristine air
> it twirls around the mountain.

64

Kōan (4)

Great compassion will disperse even the darkest cloud. This is the true imperative. This is the great teaching. One who has the single eye is about to enter nirvana. Novice, drag that rotting corpse out of here.

Case:

Tsung Men taught the assembly saying, "Within nothingness there is a road out of the dust. Forever and ever this has been shown to the people."
A monk asked, "Does this mean everywhere, or nowhere?"
Tsung Men replied, "Like a good horse, go when you see the shadow of the whip."

Notes:

1. Above is cloudy sky, below is brown earth. This is everyone's concern.
2. To a quick horse, one blow will suffice.
3. To look is easy, to see very hard.
4. When pressed, the novice frowns.

Commentary:

Compassion gives entry to those who seek. This has nothing to do with the whip. For one with a single eye, delusion scatters.

Verse:

> Tied as he is to this world,
>   he grasps at air
>
> Then strips down
>   every flowering branch
>   to make a whip.

Kōan (5)

Pointer:

So, so; not so, not so. In the midst of a struggle, both sides become valuable. Moving forward, even the tortoise leaves traces with his tail. Moving backward, the shrinking spirit finds safety with the hermit. If, on the other hand, you neither move forward nor backward, how will the falcon eat?

Case:

Fa Chou encountered a hermit on the road. "What are you boiling in that broken-legged pot?"
The hermit shook his wooden spoon and shouted.
Fa Chou said, "Are those wild greens?"
Again, the hermit raised his spoon and shouted.
"After three or four shouts, what then?" asked Fa Chou.
The hermit, having nothing more to say, offered Chou his bowl.

Notes:

1. Look! A falcon is roosting on his outstretched hand.
2. Worms and maggots crawl downward into the dirt.
   Everything has a direction.
3. There is no value in the fourth cut.
4. With practice you will learn to swallow your voice.

Commentary:

Sometimes a stranger on the road will have a snake's head but a dragon's tail. For the rest of his life, he will have conflict. Do not enter into his confusion. In an argument, each occupies a pivotal position. Staying in one place is more example than principle.

Verse:

Two shouts—
the sound of thunder
crosses the sky.

Kōan (6)

<u>Pointer:</u>

If you add error upon error, you are not yet an adept. If you take up two but let three go, you are in the same pit. You know, there's more to this than surface.

<u>Case:</u>

When Tung Yen was living in a hut, he spent his days clapping to the rhythm of dripping water. A traveler passing by heard him and asked, "Why don't you fix that leaking roof?"
Yen replied, "One hand presses down, one hand lifts up."

<u>Notes:</u>

1. Those who know the tune are few.
2. Ask one, answer eight.
3. Seeing fault, he loses sight of the teaching.
4. It won't do to let the error go.

<u>Commentary:</u>

If two are in the same pit, the dirt doesn't change. Those who only ask questions pile one error on top of another. His tongue falls to the ground. Where is there to go? Once again, he has lost sight of his staff.

<u>Verse:</u>

> One eye on what is above,
> > the other on what is below.
>
> Though the frog leaps
> > he can't get out of the basket.

Kōan (7)

<u>Pointer:</u>

Earth one day, heaven the next; heaven one day, winter after that. It's like cutting a skein of thread: if one is cut, all are cut. When all the stars go dark, the sun and moon will follow. Still, life and death must amount to something. To test, I cite this: look!

<u>Case:</u>

A monk asked Grand Master Yen, "If the wind responds equally in all ten directions, how will I find the way?"
Master Yen said, "Today, I am tired and cannot explain for you. Go ask Ta Tou."
When the monk asked Ta Tou, Tou said, "Why not ask the Teacher?" The monk replied,
"The Teacher sent me here to ask you." Tou furrowed his brow. "This headache will not let me think. If you want an answer, try Elder Brother Hsueh."
When the monk went to Hsueh and asked his question, Hsueh said, "Even after snapping my fingers on the mountain, I do not understand."
The monk related this to Grand Master Yen who said, "Tou is trailing mud; Hsueh is dripping rain."

<u>Notes:</u>

1. Even snapping his fingers did not make him wake up.
2. Where did he get this question?
3. The treasury of teachings cannot prevent the monk from binding himself with straw ropes.
4. He should have pressed Master Yen. Stumbling past, he forgot to follow the road.
5. There's a stone bridge and a log bridge. Some choose the Path. Others choose the Great Way.

Commentary:

If the wind responds equally in ten directions, the answer should be clear. The monk muddies his shoes by asking all these questions. Isn't it obvious by now? East gate, west gate, south gate, north gate.

Verse:

> A master painter dips his brush
> > so he might swim
> > > naked in a mountain stream:
>
> There
> > where the heavens hang,
> > > where the slanting sun will set.

IV

Consider Pa Ling

Under a pale veil of moonlight
     a white horse
          enters the white flowers.

In an instant, winter arrives.

Scuplted by fog
     a swan floats through
          a bed of silvery reeds

bending seed tips
     this way and that.
          The world is not hidden.

Perfect equanimity:
     A mouthful of frost?
          A scattering of clouds?

Check!

So keen is our desire
     this patch-robed monk
          spent decades

piling snow
     fine as rice powder
          into an alabaster bowl.

Consider Nan Feng

Reddened by a raw wind,
his face cannot express
the wild place he has landed.
Winter's sharp sword
points the way till he finds a place
where he can turn himself around.

North of the river, snow.

South of the river, more snow.

In the distance, layers of cloud-topped rocks,
the high hurdles of an alpine ascent.

Heedless of the drifts, the skeletal,
bone-white birch, he trudges
tirelessly toward those steep peaks:

one foot and then the next
and then another and the one
after that.

Emptiness is boundless

so to lose the path
frees him in every direction.

Consider Fa Sou

In a clear mirror
the whistling arrow
shoots right back.

It is a great teacher
who corners you with the truth.

Having said this much,
the second arrow strikes deep.

This is not to be taken lightly.

The darting fish
penetrates the glass surface,
the iron shield.

Sometimes a thought gets through.

Wind follows the tiger.
Clouds follow the wind.

Consider Wu Chou

To this very day
   a monk
      sleeps in the fields.

The wind blowing cannot enter.

What temple is this?

It is laughable,
   but there's no visible
      sword inside his laughter.

Near a spreading patch
   of purple-headed thistle,
      he tests his resolve.

His tea bowl falls to the ground.

Though there's barely a sound when it breaks,
   a man with a thousand hands
      could not count the pieces.

Consider Lin Shan

Inside his words
   whichever way they move
      the rainy days continue.

Now, the slick pavement shimmers
   pearl-gray as a herring scale.
      Riches of the language.

The storm draws a breath.

Across the southern sky,
   sheet lightning. As if a chill wind
      amid that drumming downpour,

amid the dimpled creek water,
   could stop. As if a puddle
      could be spoken aloud.

Consider Yung Wu

When water rises
he loses his nostrils,
but the boat rides high.

If he loses his nostrils,
his eyes are gone, too.

His feet are frantic;
ten fingers, flapping.

At first this is news.
Later, this is also news.

In the light of sparks
struck from stone,
thirty blows of inspiration.

Consider Lu Chang

Does Chang feel his teeth falling out?
One... two... three...

His mouth shuts.

How will he speak?

Like the moon
released at last and speechless,
he has lost his descendants.

Life splits—
a rift, a cleft, the half-
light between waking and sleeping.

A quartz-colored dawn rescues him.
The day clears.
Dizzy waves rush to shore.

The factory calls him to work, but
even there, the gap-toothed

partitions in the wall
where their rice bowls are kept

stay empty. It's another
sad round of layoffs.

How many more will be lost?
How many?

Consider Ma Jen

Two hands but three faces.
Such is my life.

Courting a lump of dirt.
Courting a flute with no holes.

There's a thorn in the soft mud of my heart
so tonight I pick up my pen.

But don't go into this ghost cave
if you need to make a living.

Consider P'an Lin

Thirty loads of mud.
I'll wear out my straw sandals.

The first road is low.
The second one is narrow.

Always there are obstacles.
Even the master's pen leaks.

Thus, I cut off the flow of my thoughts
without keeping a single drop.

Sitting cross-legged, I wash
black ink from a black lacquer bucket.

Consider Pau Cho

Discontent begins with a warning.
On nights such as this, he sits
meditating in a mountain cave,
a congregation of one.

Hoisting a lightning bolt to his brow,
he takes charge of the situation.
Thunder rumbles along his lips.
Darkness thrashes him, but he bends,
a bare-armed tree in the wind.

Cho could sit there until his legs
crumbled to dust.
Try as he might,
he has yet to reach nirvana.
At first he cannot get there.
Afterward, he goes too far.

Consider Tzu Kuan

For his part, hours of wavering.

Thoughts come and go like butterflies,

flitting from milkweed to marigold,
cornflower to clover.

They carry their delicacy
wherever they go.

Or like feathers lost in a berry bush,
syllables drift to the ground.

Something catches in his throat.

Twilight watches him and waits.

Where did the day go?

When an unexpected crow lands,
thick as a drop of ink,

he returns to the world.

With clear letters the world fills
with his unfinished thoughts.

Consider Yun Men

For every drop of water, a drop of ice.
What does the sky say?

I, for one, have doubts about this.

The four seasons will not turn from our questions.
A thousand sages cannot leap past this.

Six do not take it in.

Thus, it is said: The eye of reality has no flaws.
Why raise waves where there is no wind?

V

In the Deserted Hour

Not those on their knees
        anxious as moths
                whirling around every streetlamp.

Not those
        who *breed like flies*
                as Saint Augustine said

or those with stone ears
        holding stone harps
                as you walk through a garden.

Neither those insubstantial as ether
        nor the combative ones
                drawn to the armies of God.

Not even the stylized one
        who climbed down
                from heaven's heights to reach me.

No,
        none of these
                belong in the deserted hour

when all hope is lost,
        when one follows
                the receding world

the way meadow grass
        bows before
                an evening wind.

On that day, let me remember
  those brought near—
      winged creatures—
          onto the fields of praise.

Misfortune

A house is measured by language.
I have Mandelstam with me in my bed;
The imprisoned words he once hid
Tucked inside a coffee pot, I keep
Next to me when I sleep. Without him,
I could not bear my loneliness for long.

The Russians have always understood.
Misfortune multiplies like wildflowers
Until there's a memorial garden in every vase.
My room is overrun with color.
That's how poetry arrives:
One death, two; three deaths, four.

Because a Father is Like a God

I bow to the river
      hauling itself
            headlong into a narrow gorge

I bow to waterfalls cascading
      over polished walls of rock
            those steep unstable slopes

I bow to the falling curtain of rain
      the habits of perception
            to that belt of blue-needled spruce

I bow to the years I walked
      the ridge's knife-edge path
            without you

Because a father is like a god
      and a god is always filled
            with power he dispenses

I bow to the plummeting ravines
      the perilous spine of cliffs
            every cloud-wrapped cave

Hemmed in by a protruding
      granite slab on one side
            a foaming cauldron on the other

I bow
      to the world unfallen
            when you died

To the gun shot
      exploding through thorn bushes
           and towering thistle

Suspended between earth and sky
      between drifting mist
           and precipitous drop

I bow to Rilke's angels
      who break us open
           out of who we are

I bow to the one who divides
      who will and who will not
           be refined by suffering

On this gravel mat
      clapped against
           a limestone ledge

I bow as I always do
      to the crumbling temple
           I made of you

To the Birds of Spring

Poignant the meaning of spring birds

To the birds of spring, to their songs in the air,
to grassy nests built high in dead trees,
to the downy woodpecker, the common redpoll,
to the nuthatch and the orange-loving oriole,
to every feathered thing that shakes its wings
or hangs upside down from a crooked branch,
to the great blue heron who glides to a landing
near a bulging river, to the low-flying hawk,
the crimson cardinal, to the glorious green hillside
where I walk, to the crisp clanging of the bells,
the heavy, priestly cows, black and white
as my mother's flowered cotton, to the pleasure of her voice
and the clear light that surrounds her, to the repetition of this season
so I can greet her on a day such as this
in everything—because it is not what I look at
but what, after years without her, I see.

A Face Comes Up

wedged in a muddy bank
above the river-wash

a rock big
as a baby's head

a face comes up
out of it

a mottled cheek
mossy cap of hair

a vein-thin crack
that squirms into a lip

my fingers touch
what's unbidden

in its faint
hieroglyphic frown

pass over the grainy
stain of its nostrils

cannot stop polishing
the sallow sockets

two smooth grooves
where eyes should have been

in the beginning it is said
the world was covered with water

and the great creator
dwelt deep in a rock

so when I unearth
the granite skull

when my hands discover
half its head is gone

the left side caved in
I bend without thinking

bend to the riverbed
let it sink

face-down as the current
slides past flowing

downstream carrying leaves
broken sticks

long-tailed clouds
the world water again

pouring forth
over the one I let

slip back
into that lucent wavering.

One Thought Attracts Another

1.

Thin-bodied and hollow
        but dangling,

untouched by wind
                but bound,

hundreds of sapling-like shoots
        tap against the window.

        Not so far a way
witch-hazel, wood sorrel, foam flowers
                erupt near the river.

A conspicuous hawk
        —restless
                hungry—
careens overhead
        against a changing harmony of clouds.

2.

The sky weighs on me.

Churning at the horizon,
        storm clouds
                that never lose their way.

They are sure of their short lives.
They do not complain.
They live with the expectation of disturbance.

Look around:
the charged air,
the thirsty earth.

   3.

Like a flag in a storm
      the wheat field changes direction
            as a sharp wind pushes through,

sings along the fence wire,
      becomes the song
            while an unexpected

flash of lightning
      adorns
            the northern sky.

   4.

Against a leaden sky
      a filigree of leafless branches.

My eye is on the poisonous plants—
      sheep laurel, water hemlock, belladonna.

My eye is on the leaves—
      bristle-tipped, cork-winged, fan-lobed.

I applaud the green foliage of our language.

Who knows what we'll find on the other side?

This is the fugue that repeats then crumbles:
      our numbered days,
            death's ashen spark.

A branch becomes a vein.

A spider embellishes its web.

This rain is ruin and our ruin rides.

But after days of it,
        after the serpentine
                passages of water dry,

after marsh marigolds and wild violets,
        up come the moon-faced sunflowers
            drunk with light.

Reverie

splashed with light
       half the western wall
the day tilting toward the horizon

       an open curtain
            the window sees through me

an open shelf of water
       clapping waves
            a gull's cry blowing away like a sail

on the hardwood floor
       a woven carpet
            threads that make up a life

sun stretches across the bed
       warm as a lover's body
            the watery slap of memory
                my unhurried breath
inside a cocoon
       silken wings lift
            as solace emerges
its whiteness lighter than air

time sleeps
       as if this could go on forever

on the bedstand
       a cobalt vase
            a crown of clipped flowers

I breathe in a burst of color
            awareness so keen
                        I am not prepared

for the harbor bell
            or that last strand of sunlight
                        angling off a boat

before it sinks
            fathoms deep
                        as if it were inside me

Cosmic Dance

The waxing
    light of a pendent moon,
        slipping in and out of view,

shimmers silvery white,
    elemental as mercury
        or the semen of Shiva.

Dark as a doll's eye,
    the world dances
        with the alchemist above,

the god of vertigo whirling—
    four arms
        undulating in four directions,

his left foot raised,
    the right one triumphing
        over the crumpled body

we call illusion/attachment/ignorance,

his matted locks
    disheveled within
        fire's sovereign arch.

Woven into his hair,
    the holy Ganga
        released and flowing,

sinuous as the snakes that uncoil
      again and again
            with every turn.

The universe
      tilting on its axis,
            charred and expanding,

vibrates before me, spins—
      the pulse of creation
            throbbing in my ear.

The Way Back

A syrupy rope of honeysuckle

      hangs

            indecently over my head

      desire

without   a hidden   shadow

So naked a moment—then

ragged scraps of clouds

a leaf-streaked street

      the sky knitted with stars

Not the end

      but ending

The moon officiates...

How long it's taken to find a way back

Between near and far—

inexplicabilis

inextricabilis—

it's been a riddle

traversed in the dark

＊

After the cave tunnel

the yawning   unseen chasm

after the space

fracture cleared inside of me

the forbidden terrain   the uncharted center

after the linear path

the circular pattern

after the grim, private ritual of death

the compass broken   the needle static

after the rhythmic order of it all

after grief became a bird   thieving the air

dropping its seed   so that the tree would thrive

after all of this   after seeing the crescent moon

formed by the bull's horns before me

when another door opened

how willingly I walked through it

Notes

Forse che sì, forse che no: "Maybe yes, maybe no." On the wooden ceiling of a room in the fifteenth-century section of the ducal palace in Mantua is a square Roman-style labyrinth on which this text is repeated again and again.

mourning is disordered: Keith Waldrop, "First Draw the Sea," The House Seen from Nowhere, Litmus Press, 2002.

If you have not entered the dance, you mistake the event: St. John at Ephesus.

The same hell/Wherever you start from: Donald Revell, "Anaxagorus," Pennyweight Windows: New and Selected Poems, Alice James Books, 2005.

certain things have to be 'undergone': Jorie Graham, "Little Exercise," Overlord, Harper Collins, 2005.

Dear God, what is there to do...: Orhan Pamuk, The Black Book, Vintage International, 2006.

the dirt unceasingly does my thinking: John Cage, Silence: Lectures and Writitngs by John Cage, Wesleyan University Press, 1973.

in bonam/malam partem accipere aliquid: "to take a thing in good/bad part."

versantem turbine leti: "the whirly whirl of death" (Catullus).

what you depart from is not the way: Ezra Pound, Pisan Canto LXXIV, The Cantos of Ezra Pound, New Directions, 1948.

One jar of honey for the gods/One jar for the keeper of the maze: An inscription found on a clay tablet dating to ca. 1400 BCE records this votive offering from or at Amnisos. John Chadwick, The Mycenaean World, Cambridge University Press, 1976.

Kōans 1-7: See The Blue Cliff Record, tr. Thomas Cleary and J.C. Cleary, Shambhala, 1992.

Poignant the meaning of spring birds: Anon., Tr. Ronald C. Miao, Sunflower Spendor: Three Thousand Years of Chinese Poetry, Wu-Chi Liu and Irving Yecheng Lo, eds., Indiana University Press, 1975.

This rain is ruin and our ruin rides: Weldon Kees, "Variation on a Theme by Joyce," The Collected Poems of Weldon Kees, University of Nebraska Press, 2003.

inexplicabilis...inextricabilis: difficult to enter and difficult to leave

Acknowledgments

[now begins]: *Poetry International*, Vols. 18-19, October, 2012.

[how much of the map]: *Glint Literary Journal*, Issue 3, June, 2012.

[rain frog thorn bug tent bat]: Published under the title "Labyrinth" in *Ploughshares*, Spring, 2009.

Consider Pa Ling: Anthologized in *Migrations: Poetry and Prose for Life's Transitions*, Wildwood Press, 2011.

Misfortune and A Face Comes Up: *Hometown Focus*, Winter/Spring, 2012.

To the Birds of Spring: *String Poet*, Volume 1 Issue 1, May, 2011.

Because a Father is Like a God: *Poetry City, U.S.A.*, Volume Two, Spring, 2012.

One Thought Attracts Another: *The Thunderbird Review*, Volume 1, Spring, 2013.

The Way Back: *Taos Journal of International Poetry & Art*, Issue 5, 2014.

About the Author

A native of Minnesota, Francine Sterle holds an MFA degree in poetry from Warren Wilson College and has studied writing in a variety of settings, including Oxford University, Spoleto Writers' Workshop, Bread Loaf Writers' Conference, Squaw Valley Community of Writers, and the Atlantic Center for the Arts. She has three previous collections: *The White Bridge* (Poetry Harbor, 1999), *Every Bird Is One Bird* (Tupelo Press, 2001), and *Nude in Winter* (Tupelo Press, 2006). She lives in Iron, Minnesota, on the West Two River.

David Martinson–Meadowhawk Prize

To honor the life and poetry of David Martinson (1946–2010), author of *Bleeding the Radiator* (Dacotah Territory, 1974), *A Cedar Grew from His Forehead* (Loft Lecture, 1976), *Strips and Shavings* (Truck Press, 1978), and *Hinges* (Aluminum Canoe, 1996), Red Dragonfly Press has established the David Martinson–Meadowhawk Prize for a new collection poetry. Awarded annually beginning in 2013.

When the heron led me high above the water
I never once looked back.

Prize winners:

2013 *Patches of Light* by Chad Hanson

2014 *What Thread?* by Francine Sterle